T0117599

HEX & HOWL

HEX & HOWL

SIMONE MUENCH + JACKIE K. WHITE

www.blacklawrence.com

Executive Editor: Diane Goettel
Chapbook Editor: Kit Frick
Book Design: Amy Freels
Cover Design: Richard Every
Cover Art: "Untitled (Sisters in Fur Coats with Birds)" by Daisy Patton. Used with permission.

Published 2021 by Black Lawrence Press.
Printed in the United States.

Contents

Duologue

(cento with lines from Simone Muench + Jackie K. White)

Let us rewind and revel
that we are women speaking in the dark.

Let the lungs fill till transparent.
Reach, reach, we want to say

with honey and history, and so the girl
feeds the submerged surging:

lacquered, damp and deep pink, pomegranate
underneath an autumn-frosted Florida spring.

In a world sketched on a wing,
it is difficult not to fall under the spell

but we spin in reverse of every old script and cycle.
Amid wreckage, bed of wet petals, the unsaid,

we linger, saying we want more:
the windows are waking us.

I.

Hex & Howl

You studied the orange girls, cinema
gazes, wounded bodies, and angles
that wolves unbend. I looked through the eyes
of chameleons, the nightmare houses they

inhabited with crystalized skins: pebbled
and primordial, shedding their way into
waking. You and I were told to swallow
our hexed howling, refuse the reptilian

and the mammalian, unless it's tame,
you know, cow-eyed, with a roundness eager
for petting. Now we do the refusing; now

we flame in the celluloid dark, a primal
rewinding where the wolf and the lizard
let loose the elemental code to our riling.

Salt Lick

The deer wants to be iris; the iris,
glass, but the glass is a licked orange,
unsalted. All things remain separate—
us, too. All things fill themselves

with longing. Because the glass remains
iris-empty, my hands reach deer-ward,
toward salt lick and cloud, the edge
of field, its horizon of white irises,

petticoat pretty but bleached of color
like orange pith. Bearded blooms
fragile as blown glass. We are less
delicate though also leeched

and licked. A gestalt of raw.
Our rind peeled back with pining.

Against Teleology

They made Eve an event, a teleology
we've teethed too many mouths upon, jawing
uneven through supposed apple skin. We've
seeded and ceded enough. Enough gnawing

on our bones by canonized men. Let fang
become fallout, reverse this ache, this *sorry*.
Let bees shimmer inside our eyes instead
of men's glory. Let's mouth a modern story,

revise every exodus, each line of dread
they put upon us in sackcloth or satin.
We took the garden with us, now the gavel

is our godhead. We'll not be suckled or bled
to ghosts again. We're the heart's rattle,
razored at our core. Full of sharp. Full of sheen.

Portrait as Landscape: Dear Dark Garden

Outside, lining the hushed front yard,
dogwood and cherry blossoms peak
to petal cascades, hiding more basement
girl-held horrors. The pastoral says nothing

of rot. The suburban silent about ruin.
But the girls speak—of shatter, of strangle.
Of broken teeth, of more danger. The body
bent acutely into shame. *Dear dark garden,*

where you buried me, where you watched my bare
feet slipping, his ropy arms grabbing, his full
body falling on my trunk, breaking limbs
with an inarticulate hiss, say now how I was

blackened under shovel, crushed into loam.
Backyard afterlife, a new rage, an old, old wrong.

Department of Brokenness

The desert is an armory of black tires.
Assemble the animals. Assemble
the murder ballads, and the trembling
shadows. Silence strung along barbed wire

catches the heat, the threat against flesh,
and starts to hum. Always the eye believes
human forms will emerge, some voice
will clear debris, give way to a hint of light.

Instead, fading notes, roadkill. A mass
of songless bodies trussed tight with shoulder
holsters. The weathervane no longer moves,
the land is out of breath. Assemble

every muted scarecrow. Every body's
just as frail, and even the silence lies.

Portrait as Landscape: In This Grim Play

Listen to the wilderness as it sighs
under its forest of bones. So many
beings buried here: carcasses licked
back to bare anatomy. So many

epithelial cells shed: forearms, thighs,
the brush or scratch from human or tree
or thorn. So many voices cut, crypted
sky-wide or swamp-deep. Still not enough

forewarning in this grim play. The chronic
coldness of this grove is more than a composite
of moss, fox, mold. Listen to its articulations

as they accordion a history, a litany of the frail
we failed to help unfold into fierceness.
So many bright flowerings forfeited.

Mutations

Once upon a mother there was shimmer,
blue ash mirror frosted into smear. The dusk
smokes, draws mothering to mutate—
a smear sucking you under fresh blue smoke.
Once mother shimmer, once blue ash, once
frost mirrored into smear. Dusk draws down,
mothering mutates, re-draw yourself: frost
faced, mirrored eyes smeared to ashen hue.

Then draw upon a shimmer, a mother blued
to dusky ash in a frosted past till smoke
and shimmer mutate, become your mother's
mother. Drawn out into the blue-bit dusk,
smoke the shimmer, smear ash into the mirror
of frosted blues. Nothing left to draw or lose.

Solve for X

Everything is loss and the longing for
connection, but the ache of vacancy
has no home. Brittle stem flower, headless,
every planted thing knows its own uprooting,
knows that this is the way we wound:
sometimes a needle, sometimes a shovel.
Morning's wasp-bright sting turns bodies
to stories of wreckage, of folly, the dull

thudding steps we plot for going on.
If salve or salvage exist somewhere,
do the stories weave what leads us there
away from the garden's rot, obit, subplot,
toward something less dark? Not quite song
or sugar water, but a wrought ripe, sunlit.

Recast

Loss enters stage left in the form of violins
thrumming the past into forecast: mulberries
in the backyard, first time, a cushioned mess
of mauve stain, bruising caress, then forgivings.

Loss is a severed finger sent spinning
into the lake, the sun magnifying
a ring's opal fire and its milky insistence
that we break everything we love, the way

I broke apart the carnation corsage,
the way you broke my bargaining lips
on the belt buckle gift. A guitar meant

for crooning becomes a life untuned,
a molded fruit. We can't recast ruin.
We have to sit in the wound. Survive it.

Pressed

On a sheetless mattress, immobile and
undone, I was marked for ruin. I drowned
in dread, became a stain, a container
of shatter, of "I don't matter." I'm told to
muzzle that memory with pillow plush,
and smother all the old mouths' carping
as I'm pressed into performance, pushed to play
that old game perfectly. Now, I turn the mouth

into spewing glass. The anatomy of a rupture.
I burn. I bellow. I say no I say no I say no.
This is the season of the scalpel, not nostalgia.
This is the year of scraping out hauntings.
I said no. Now I shove that ghost into the fold,
press back, iron the sheets of my choosing.

II.

Self-Portrait Lined by Emily Dickinson

I measure every Grief I meet
as if I could tether it, tune it,
fair weather it—successor
to loss, where cobweb
& feather are sewn together,

where barb & bramble tattoo
untruths to the wound's
memory of a body gone. Debt
hisses like a mocking breeze
through spring with its thorny

harness. You can try to bracket it,
ration it, ladle it as though a briny
broth of stinging nettle & crushed
bees. No matter. It's venom's
slow dive, a rockbound flight

we can't ever name. They were wrong
about the ephemeral: it dilates
within, makes us vagrants, scavenging
debris, hungry, & sheltering in dead
leaves, in the warm mulch the dead leave.

Self-Portrait Lined by Alejandra Pizarnik

I am sad in the night of wolf fangs,
subdued by a heat so fleshy
it could be a dying animal, could

breed with its own seething,
then eat its young and still sink
into extinction. If breeze, if light

can't teethe this melancholy
into a new folio of beaming, then
what of singing?—when bleeding

marks the skin into a new map,
what crawling forward, to where?
I seek a cool to suck in against

this furred humidity, depression's
cleaver. A rot that can't be seen or
sung into ether as I sketch

outlines of a different being, one
more than mouth, the feral eased.
But day will come, I'll creep

quieter than a birdwatcher beyond
this body's bruised cartography, its
broken tongue, toward the tender hum.

Self-Portrait Lined by Eavan Boland

I want to know how it happened that those days
of bloom closed down into shadow. I want
to hold my sickness as though a waxen insect
fastened under glass, a found and foreign thing

to be studied with its wholeness intact. If I look
long enough, will it take on the shape of petals
or scalpels? Will it carry my reflection or mutate
into a thorned beast? Will my veins be respun

as red ivy budding in the cracks of my body
and not be shredded frail as chaff? Each minute
fills with audible exhale, an effort at singing
into the feracious flowering beyond my heaving.

Better to burn it all clear—forest, furrow,
and garden. *There will be no obituary.*

Self-Portrait Lined by Maxine Kumin

With vodka and ice, our words like living meat
meld from one set of skeleton and skin
into a fermentation that misleads, a slur
sliding my body sideways as if I were

a beekeeper and you a photograph
of scorched prairie strewn with glittering
martini glasses. We've been submerged
by a flash flood of dinner parties, guests

to our own decoupling, everyone else mesh-
masked, hazard-suited, dummy-posed.
Honeysuckle stings the humid air as if
henbane, punctuating what we don't say:

there is no cooling what touch sets the tongue
to sear, no rephrasing the under hum.

Self-Portrait Lined by Anna Akhmatova

The secret of secrets is inside me again
spooling its prickly threads into a twine
threat, a hanging loop, or a cordon

of light around my neck as I rise, shedding
the evening from my sleeves. Asking myself,
am I the outline or the interior? Or an offering

between, like a mannequin draped each day
in another's making, with a makeshift
face, open-palm gesture, a kind of heft

against hopelessness—a supplication
to the sun gods who lead a veiled dance,
braiding shadow to silhouette, eyelet

to hook. The more the exterior resembles
the delicacy within, the quieter I can keep it,
or choose to let it rustle like a silk lining

while my silence shirrs the incandescent
curve of skin, hips wreathed in porch light.
A gold earring glitters against the dusk:

I am leaning forward into the hush, spooling
loose again, from limb and cloth and land—
I cannot tell if it is the day or the world ending.

Self-Portrait Lined by Coral Bracho

Through the tremor spiked with smoke and flowers,
through the murmur, through the orchard,
we churned those ashed hours into aurora

then let its coral drape into blue-laced afternoon.
We lingered, then; the round table garnished
with carafe, clear goblets, and our oval mouths

choreographed to quietness. Our fingers
spooning the crystalline glitter as light
flashed against glass. Beyond the lemon grove,

cities pulsed, spewing grays and shadowing
every pocket-squared garden. We had the sense
that only dusk lived there, so we kept our gaze

on the galaxy of citrus swelling its yellow
presence against a sky that swelled too
into a beryl blue electricity. Though blighted,

this is the only world we may ever have.
In it, we decant the red, follow the strands
of light *that we bear in our hands like a realm.*

Self-Portrait Lined by Rosario Castellanos

I am from a far shore, from another region,
storied in a language of brine-slick stone.

Here, sunk in the evening's socket, moths
whir, marking the dark with a discordant beauty.

Everything else has stopped. Night has sewn
the wind into a funeral wrap, and the dawn

will drown itself in a pastel smear. No traveler
is a narrative unto herself. Each with sentences

searing, curses thrown over shoulders like spit-
flecked salt. Here, scars sharpen into basalt

pretending to mask the marring with shine
like a lure meant to disguise its danger,

but I carry a landscape sketched from a lexicon
written into my skin. The margins extending

toward a bright-edged cartography,
a late voyage beyond wreck into revival.

III.

Disclosure

but dresses dressed in dresses are dresses—Saeed Jones

The dress says I will frame your beauty
when I bury you. The dress is a chateau
of ghosts demanding don't go, don't love
your nakedness. It is the vehicle, the volta

that comes too soon, without steering, only
sash for a wheel. Let it fly loose, grip yourself.
The dress is a thief laced with history's lies.
Your beauty needs no frame; pivot on this

exposé as the body drowns its cargo
of blues beneath a voluminous red dress
that enters the room before you do.
Let it go on ahead, swirl its cliché, evoke

whatever gazes it can. That nakedness
you love refigures any space you choose.

Objection

Some wept watching *Love Connection*. Some
wept in search of goddesses. Some wept
early in the year. Some wept later in a novel
with faces reflected in a pool of vodka.

Some were warned by lipstick on the glass.
Some did the warning by earmarking odd
pages. Some whispered ancient spells,
some wrote coded scripts. All were rejected.

But some rose saying *no longer* between
lightning's flash & clap. Some rose to mistrial.
Some rose to file a missing persons report.
Some rose & cast curses, till all mouths licked

in spit, & fingers pointed, unpricked. Their arms
tort-wielding, eyes tearless and daring: watch *this*.

Queue

Cue the shimmering footage of girls
in white stockings strolling for orange sodas.
Then cue them to shred the sepia vestiges
of skirts once swinging like chandeliers.

Cue them to kick off boots to syrupy tunes
in every gin joint and change up the genre.
Jazzed up or country swung, let's all croon
a new juke box: euphony not eulogy, loud

but not lewd. Let's unscrew the stage lights,
sing adieu to blank cartridges, beer coasters,
and tequila-gold walls riddled with peepholes.

We've recalled the chorus line, unbolted
the poles. We know how to let loose on our own
terms, tango or two-step, and in our own time.

Portrait as Landscape: Of Grisly, of Lovely

A girl is both tiara and shadow,
a boarded-up window, a wooded ravine.
Neither scar nor slit, but a garnet
of grisly, of lovely, of lonely,

plumbed and deeply plumbing shine.
A girl is also substance and pluck,
a crowbar, a prying, and a peering into
the ugly, the empty, silt and stone.

Less paper doll, more shadow shifter, full
of foghorn and ghost glitter. Petal-
precious and profane, a canted frame.

She is skiff and sky. Fox-gloved meadow.
Pinwheel and rope jumped over, jumped
through. Mock curtsy chilled and scissor kick.

Portrait as Landscape: Not the Fox

She was wronged, flung from childhood
into a vista of fox bones under forest moss.
Was she blue aura or gold ore—a myth
of the river, a silhouette in the mirror?

She was thronged by norm-chatter and dank
hisses, others' wishes warping her girlhood
with crushes and carrion. Could she cut
the shadow, re-smelt a core, smudge their glass?

She is tired of being frame and folly.
She wants to be the buzzard not the dead fox,
the boat's bow cutting a path through fast water,
the bright glint of the scythe singing prairie.

She imagines herself moving through the tall grass,
through the pond's stillness, beyond glass into exhalation.

Portrait as Landscape: Shell Game

She's silk static   and wetsuit smooth.
A shawl of dark water,   opaque glass.
Comet, eclipse,   fiery veil, a sealed record.
Add gloss to gumption,   and she'll be

plum-sauce sweet   machete ready.
A tactician of ephemera,   her sass tapes
shut any ask.   She stirs up operatic scat.
She's divested,   self-vetted, barefoot

at the dance,   not prince-seeking.
Not numb or succumbing,   not red feather
lure, but the line.   The measure of her fervor
has never been met.   Too many

contradictions? Or just adept   shape-shifter,
giving the slip to swindlers, the game   rearranged.

From a Grimoire

We dance the moon hours dusk struck,
a smear of mulberry on winter birch.
We become a gothic novel, black
lace over bird cage. Swirling a glass

of claret as cobwebs slip into gray
macramé. We know the screech owl
means to harmonize with the needle
scratching on that old phonograph

of body, its croon gone crone, gone
cored. An Adam's apple of curses,
scars that resemble the edges
of a blood-slick abattoir. Our mouths

ripen with wine, night animals, flowers,
as we slip off the human and prowl.

Rebuttal

Against the grinding fever of suppressed
song, against a muzzle's searing, sound
is a muscle.   The body's rebuttal,

a kind of clamoring
held to seethe. Against siren-women, against

cliché's cacophony, we keep spinning, spooling
counterpoint, contrapuntal, the contraband
of roots, radical, fractal, optional, historical—

Drink this. Sing this: our tongues will not be bridled
as though miniature ponies put out to pasture.
Nor will our tales be jeered as old-wives' blather.

Against *hush-hush, tsk-tsk*, we stream melodies
through barbed wire even when vexed, breathless
as popped balloons.   Even then

our sound surges through
hex   into galloping hymn.

Coda

Fingering old flesh wounds, false starts
assail you. It's autumn. All we invent
is another ending. Yellow singes orange
scraping the blistered rage. That old palette

of ruby rust. You said *no*, he said *yes*. Your voice
weighed less. But it stayed, darkening the curtains
of that house where each room was a contusion
built of disillusion. Leaves pressed like hands

in that familiar gray smear, like test splotches
splayed on sterile white. You tongue bite
to keep the anger they want from becoming
ochre revelation, then let open the gash.

For you are the coup de grace, the gas fire:
the red conclusion to autumn's impasse.

Acknowledgments

Cincinnati Review: "Portrait as Landscape: Not the Fox"

Denver Quarterly: "Mutations"

Ecotone: "Queue"

The Hopkins Review: "From a Grimoire"

Hobart: "Rebuttal"

Hypertext Magazine: "Portrait as Landscape: In This Grim Play," "Portrait as Landscape: Dear Dark Garden," and "Recast"

The Journal: "Against Teleology," "Portrait as Landscape: of Grisly, of Lovely," and "Coda"

Los Angeles Review: "Self-Portrait Lined by Emily Dickinson"

RHINO: "Self-Portrait Lined by Anna Akhmatova"

Pleiades: "Pressed" and "Objection"

Posit: "Disclosure," "Department of Brokenness," and "Solve for X"

Spoon River Poetry Review: "Hex & Howl," "Portrait as Landscape: Shell Game," and "Duologue"

"Against Teleology" will appear in the anthology *Sonnets from the American: Essays and Poems*, University of Iowa Press, 2022.

"Against Teleology" will appear in the anthology *Between Paradise and Earth: Eve Poems*, Orison Books, 2021.

"Pressed" will appear in the *Processing Crisis* anthology, published by Risk Press and Saint Mary's College of California, forthcoming.

Thanks to Christine Maul Rice who nominated "Recast," published in *Hypertext*, for *Best of the Net*, 2020.

Many thanks to Daisy Patton for her generosity in letting us use her gorgeous artwork as well as Richard Every for his cover design skills. Much gratitude to Anna Maria Hong and Mary Biddinger for their stunning blurbs and support. And, of course, an exuberant thank you to the fabulousness of Kit Frick, Diane Goettel, and the entire Black Lawrence team, especially for their support of collaborative work. We would also like to acknowledge the Lewis University Faculty Scholar Award program that provided course reassignment time for this book to be completed and Dora Malech and Laura T. Smith for the opportunity to showcase our project as part of their Sonnets from the American Virtual Symposium.

Simone would also like to thank Jackie, who has been a remarkable force to work with, inspiring me and infusing my writing life with her brilliance. Many thanks to Kasia Wolny and the Wolny Writing Residency for allowing time to work on this manuscript. Much love and thanks to my friends and family whom I feel incredibly fortunate to have in my life: Richard Every, Charlotte Every, Kim Ambriz, Jessie Ambriz, Hadara Bar-Nadav, Chiyoko Yoshida, Melissa Grubbs, Sarah Long, Rebecca Morgan Frank, Beth McDermott, Lana Rakhman, Kenyatta Rogers, Dean Rader, Jen Consilio, Jason Koo, Jesse Muench, Loretta McSween, John McSween, Michael Anania, Chuck Crowder, Gary Gannaway, Bill Mondi, Lanko Miyazaki Goldberger, Stephanie McCanles, and Wesley Kimler, as well as my awesome students and *Jet Fuel Review* editors who help solidify my love of collaborative writing and teaching.

Jackie would also like to thank, first and foremost, Simone, for reigniting my active enjoyment in writing poems, and Diane Cabrera for her constant and continual encouragement and support. A shout out to my sister, Tera Mascarenas, for her curiosity and cheerleading along the way, as well as Patricia Esposito and Dana Goodman, and all the family and friends who helped in my recovery, making my making of poems again possible.

Simone Muench is the author of several books including *Lampblack & Ash* (Kathryn A. Morton Prize for Poetry and *NYT* Editor's Choice; Sarabande, 2005), *Orange Crush* (Sarabande, 2010), and *Wolf Centos* (Sarabande, 2014). Her chapbook *Trace* won the Black River Chapbook Competition (Black Lawrence, 2014), and her collection, *Suture*, is a book of sonnets written with Dean Rader (Black Lawrence, 2017). She also co-edited the anthology *They Said: A Multi-Genre Anthology of Contemporary Collaborative Writing* (Black Lawrence, 2018). Some of her honors include an NEA fellowship, three Illinois Arts Council fellowships, the Marianne Moore Prize for Poetry, and residency fellowships to Yaddo, Artsmith, and VSC. In 2014, she was awarded the Meier Foundation for the Arts Achievement Award, which recognizes artists for innovation, achievements, and community contributions. She received her PhD from the University of Illinois and is a professor of English at Lewis University where she teaches creative writing and film studies. Currently, she serves as faculty advisor for *Jet Fuel Review*, as a senior poetry editor for *Tupelo Quarterly*, and creator of the HB Sunday Reading Series.

Jackie K. White has has been an editor with *RHINO*, faculty advisor for *Jet Fuel Review*, and professor of English at Lewis University. She has published three previous chapbooks—*Bestiary Charming* (Anabiosis), *Petal Tearing & Variations* (Finishing Line), and *Come clearing* (Dancing Girl)— along with numerous single-authored poems and translations in such journals as *ACM*, *Bayou*, *Fifth Wednesday*, *Folio*, *Quarter after Eight*, *Spoon River*, *Third Coast*, *Tupelo Quarterly*, and online at prosepoem.com, seven corners, shadowbox, and superstitionreview.com, among others. An assistant editor for *They Said: A Multi-Genre Anthology of Contemporary Collaborative Writing*, her collaborative poems (with Simone Muench) have appeared in *Ecotone*, *Hypertext*, *The Journal*, *Pleiades*, and others.